Render

Gene Hult

Brighten
Press

Houston
2018

First Print Edition, 2018

ISBN 978-1-7323381-4-2

Brighten Press
Houston, Texas

info@brightenpress.com
www.brightenpress.com

Printed in the United States of America

Render

Contents

Admission

Transmission

Emission

The first section of "Five Dead Women" was published as "*from* Five Dead Women" in the *Denver Quarterly*, Fall-Winter 2002.

"Five Dead Women" and "Taliesin" were published on the *Caper Literary Journal* site in December 2010.

The text of "The Scrivener" is entirely abridged from "Bartleby, the Scrivener: A Story of Wall Street" by Herman Melville, 1853.

Admission

Taliesin

At night magic
is most often extant. Listen
for the glimmering source
of feeble rushlights while overhead
consequential formulas cycle in silence.

The Moon herself rests
upon the tangled branches of the trees—
stout vows, arguments, sighs, and threats:
oak, wailing when cut;
hawthorn, dominion of ageless,
mean, fine-featured creatures;
Northerners say ash holds up the sky;
and always, a willow, shuffling to grab
travelers to entrap within a dense trunk.

A name for the old man has been rendered
unimportant in this story.
His eyes are a boy
on a winnowing floor,
surrounded by similarity.

A moment all is still
a name invoked under the sun when words
float cheapest thistledown in a daybeam—
with only distant, maddening echoes
of the power they once possessed.

Lasting perhaps a night, words gave
shape. Knowing the name of a thing
was essence perception,
therefore a moment's mastery.
Distinguish the matter of absence—
a summons of being,
encased alive in words.

I am a composer, an artificer
like the specious mockingbird.
I amassed multitudes before my release,
I was the words in letters.

This night sings, faint in falling mists.
The ground dampens thick with wet
under an encouraging canopy of ash.

Before the sun rises with bursting light,
listen.

Five Dead Women

1. Megan loved the movies.

Feared past, at thirty-three,
the moment of plucked
from obscurity discovery,
Dame Fortune finally folded
the coverlet back. A prostitute

of golden sacrifice and secret grace,
a watershed catchment for battered
ambition. Worn shopgirl—

requirements of pink powder,
perfumed scarves, mauled lipstick,
the retail waged anointing of
wrinkle cream and toes so soft—

showgirl dreams entangled
in scented hair, phone calls
to mother the only evidence
of promise as late for the casting

couch, the call, she blow
dried her tresses in the tub.

2. Daisy, desolate from disuse,

bought kitchen appliances
with frightening frequency
as her forty-eighth birthday

flashed searing hot,
a magnesium scalpel.

"Did you miss the rain?" she asks
her apartment's swarthy underground
garageman, while exiting
to shop for a Target toaster.
"It was on the news."

The barren, treeless stretch of Route 202,
how to assuage the derailment
of genetic destiny, how to unknot
the desiccated kernels of possibility,
when time has repossessed
its Mixmaster lottery of the body?

Daisy adjusts her hairpiece
in the rearview. A child

appearance, warped in the
corner of her cornea, into
the road with Freon eyes. Heart-

leap veer, a rugged minivan.

3. Brenda was a beauty.

Her long, twenty-four-year-old
legs had a lightly sunkissed sheen,
which she buffed and polished

while the dust on her coffee table
was defiantly constant, motes tumbling

down through her studio's sunbeams
to gather around her refrigerator's
buzzing electrical coils
like a beard of bees.

The following footsteps started
in December, on lunch at the deli
under a Manhattan money hive
of dissected and teetering balances.

The invisible clattering haunted
and described her routine, her late hours,
her blithe shortcut into a darkened alley,
dazzle blinded by distant streetlamps.

Her legs intricate twitching moth wings,
a cricket's rubbed eek of vibrato,
fly legs' urgent, hungry crisscrossing,
they would smell of dewy meadows at dawn.

He revealed the desperate accountant
she'd expected. In the darkness he

was as formless as empathy. Brenda pivots
to stride, discovers his infesting friends

bewildered by a delusional and depraved
purpose of savagely primal pheromones.

4. Frederica craved the wind.

Sixteen, she remembers her mother,
but has forgotten her face and name.

She wishes wild birds to clutch
her in their talons, flapping her straining
from the ground, dangling

her wretchedness in effigy.

The night breeze disregards quiet,
demands

a blot, seeping into ruts and rivulets as
she whistled upon the hole in the flute
with fluttering fingertips and pursed lips.

Freddie stifled thick coughs to keep
from being noticed, and yet
bristles at sidelong regards,

tugging at the chafing tethers
to the torment of the actual.

The voice of whispered insinuations
caresses her ear in a hiss of unworthiness,
picking at the endless imperfections
of being encased in flesh.

A firm draft whisks her to the ledge,
earthbound cars blaring far below.

The wind overlooked or neglects
to leaven her plummet to the pavement.

5. Lauren carved glass. At eighty-
one, her breathing is harsh, shattered,
slicing trachea, bronchioles, each alveolus
with a lifespan of sharp fused sand

and obsessive dedication
settled resident in her lungs.

But the patterns her instruments
traced in the molten molecules—

refracting light in a fine, subtle bevel,
supplying shadows to circumscribe shape,
etching illustrations in the prismatic ether—
shimmer, earnestly coherent in her memory
with a consistently rediscovered
childlike delight in chromatic dispersion,
in rainbows.

The hospital sheets are crisp
on her translucent skin.
After years of repetitive, constant effort
she feels time's allowance to embrace
the authority of ease,
industry's simple, common, only
reward for work well done.

Lauren fumble slides oxygen mask off,
refusing to beep out final gasp
into plastic.

Warped, rippling with pain,
she exhales glittering hard gems
into the welcoming air.

Lazy Magician
in San Francisco

The silent birds swoop in straggly flocks
above chunky squares of skyline.
Unfinished towers. Jagged steel beams
stretch abandoned fingers
toward a drowning brown sun.

A clattering of fingers would conjure
a more aesthetic, colorful world,
another gritty reality or a fantasy
of wonder and metaphor,
a woodland boy secure in sinewy arms,
trees rustling secrets of departure,
bloody battles of inspired hordes,
a singularity cheerful with lucidity
and undiffused against a backdrop alive
with independent angels of happenstance.

Fight a notion
that begs to allow congruity
with tellers of gnomic fortunes,

salesmen pushing the oil of asps,
who turn their other cheeks
when faced with an ideal of adoration.

I'm lying on a forest green futon,
shivering in today's damp cold.
I toasted a bagel for my baby's breakfast,
and then reclined to watch
the jade plants subdividing
their spatulate thumbs
in endless expansion.

Overdramatically exhausted, a swoon
and sigh to retreat into autonomic dreams,
wholly created scintillating realms
where everyone's names are unforgotten,
and my motivations reveal their mysteries,
interrupted by the yawning of my jaw.

I will not be able to breathe
deep inhalations much longer.
How frightening it is to see
the extent of this life,
to witness its regular breadth,
and still stand on soft feet
while the unseen serpents writhe

between the molecules of plasmic amnion,
slinking for entrance, hissing when rebuffed,
coiling in constant venomous effort.

So much vegetable beauty
summons mindlessly to my touch,
the autumn colors in the deciduous forest:
plumage ornamentation embroidered
on a snuggly comforter of sacrifice
without conscious consideration,
miracles unfolding out of the dirt.

Gather at my feet
to watch me sleep.
Don't mistake my snoring rumble
for wisdom, and my somnambulant speech
is as unremembered as the Oracle at Delphi's
while she chews olive paste on toast,
wiping huffed sleep from her eyes,
breaking her hollow fast.

These tasks require
the strength of giants
only intermittently obedient to command.
The heavy lifters need cajoling,
bribery beyond my abilities to provide.

Yet the pen moves,
easing out susurrations of misdirection,
hissing lying lines of serpentine grace,
pretty approximations of creation,
while I try to steer
with one eye drowsing shut.

Wave hands over the solvent waters,
urging repast, summoning the misplaced,
as something lost surfaces, rusted
and corroded, an Atlantean city, jutting
its drying spires into the sky.

Notes from Donald Revell's Poetry Workshop

Ah . . . it keeps
you busy

Elegy: preservation of absence

arranging without ordering

Stand in front of the movement—
decentering
poet not the
center

confrontational elegy
Loss is good news in
these elegies
increase of chaos

how to show up
without being a
tyrant

wrestling with the angel—
it keeps changing—

and if you're lucky,
you lose

regretfully
staining
the silence

no emotion recollected in tranquility

departure

it could be otherwise

no innocent authority

pure event

poetry does
not exist
at the expense
of the world

tiny last resort of tremendous

elemental: element cannot be reduced
without annihilation

two things happening
without one
appropriating
the other

further reduction would be silence

any sound beyond this must be justifiable
every word is next word—no filler
unwrite world or unwrite poem
executioner or victim
poem defacing itself

damage space in which a
poem can open
wild wasting
—fractured!

a poem as a waste product
of what it was supposed to be

what's still going treeward . . .

words free to mean anew—
don't mean nothing yet

blank in a new way
getting the old meanings out—
deformation as a result of resisting closure
poetry without carnage

innocence: I do no harm

a career goal

I saw: interiorizing
moves to: I was
dislocation:
I am

drain language of motive, volition,
even presence

object asking to be witnessed
approaching poetry
by deforming perceptions

textures of shadows
words are not transparent

words are elegy to presence,
emotion

subjectivity
ability to move
the words

writing perpetuates an absence
attempt to write that which does not erase

always in the midst—
and write there!

unbinding of origins
book must drown in the world

abundance of hope
inwarding hope—
outwardly non-image

poetry making war on
the dominance of language

poetry pointing out incompetence
to the real

aspire for second-rate status

poem does not equal love
prayer does not equal God

appropriation of photographs

Barthes, *Camera Lucida*

the reader is always alive
the writer, not always

every reader response is valid

Work Sets You Free
sign on gate of concentration camp

tyrannies of syntax

commonplace book
instead of a journal

Cori's Party

We are embarrassed. Cori is
dressed up in a blue blouse,
a periwinkle girl, crumpled paper
crisp. She stands alone
on the brown-tile patio.
Her arms cover her face, hinged
over her eyes.
It's a sixth grade graduation party.

Cori's father came home fired.
He thunders, enraged, a deep ridge
digging into his forehead.

Cori's mother says, Calm down,
please cut the cake,
so he takes a rusty machete
and hacks the dessert into thin strips.

We try to eat it,
but blue icing topples
from our paper plates.

We grind it helplessly
into the flat brown grass.

Alone

The details of this muckraked existence
and the templates of prescribed worship
were at best separated at birth.

Alarmingly, my savior has revealed
himself as the virgin and the vixen,
object of reverence in spite of
the crucified lust he invites.

The Bible is another good book
in the pantheon of my shelves.
Attune to the subcutaneous resonances
of everybody's sleeping stories.
Our endings need not be as violent,
but they may be equally meaningful.

The trinity was not apt
merely for the special.
We are the wriggling tips
of pseudopodial projections
into this collective dimension.

Notice and nurture the flowers,
but do not disturb the wildlife.

Retract in ecstasy to share
with the greater churn of findings
what we alone have experienced,
but don't preach those limited perceptions.

The potency of the hookah
has not been disappointing.
Blurt oodles of nonsense,
rushing past the salient aspects
in a flush of hogwash.

I am still searching for an exact knack.

A longing of sufficient kilowattage
to cause gnawings of the windowsill
when prevented from going inside.

What do you believe in?
Don't leave me alone
adrift on this dinky dinghy
believing there is always more to believe.

Begging for the combination,
a rejection in towels,

as emaciated, taut old men
masturbate and writhe, watching
with sunken hungry eyes.
Wretched blighters I fear becoming,
flitting from the greasy shadows
to ruffle the soft leg hair
of my timidity.

My transparencies with nothing
to hide can listen to the subterranean
thump of petrified metronomes.

While we speak in symbols,
consider the validity of an ideal:
a desperate craving for example
amidst mythological murmurings of purity.

In this season of rebirth,
I reach out with tiny, diseased hands
for a jetty of reassurance,
a denial of solitary confinement.

I see you, and, unbelievably,
scoff at the vestiges of glorious grace
that streak the sunset
like orange eyelashes.

From where shall I bleed
to prove I care? Such willful
obscurity, such a mockery
of emasculated manhood.

Earnestness is not to be trusted,
but those who deny its sustenance
are alone.

Prophet

Ignorant agent of a proposed theocracy,
dispense faith in time-release capsules—
tasting savory then bitter on the tongue,
affecting a secret carnal eloquence.

Hide in a mist of dark shone sequins
a volatile spirit of unsent letters
which must dance and sing again
when refused sunlight returns.

Staring at the cosmic,
a measure piles and furs.
Immersed in the transitory,
farewell my sisters—
no constant of consensual uncertainty.

The ideal shreds, tears again,
scattering on a hot, teasing breeze,
multitudes of confetti flittering
to unforeseeably recombine.

I must know to know,
this grasped wisp of surfaced whim—

without a lie of here the simple answer
and machine is machine holy is.

Teacher, sir, release the arm
of the body.
My face grows medicinal tight.
The hour is late and cannot cut short.

I know and a man
who follows me in darkness
home from a distance
decided safe.

Transmission

Confidentially

He and I are and collide drafting snow.

Projections overlay tangles
of painful, warm illusions,
ostrich the hidden fangs—

while I want in the morning light
to be an entranced bodhisattva
who dares to read another book.

Often anger is
an indoor orchid in bloom today.
A mother of many is in a sleigh driving.
Distance and swans honking

the beauty of the mar.
I attempt to escape,
to obfuscate the obvious,
to bewilder you with squid ink,
highlighting the white.

My father has had an almost carved duck
on his workbench with one sighted eye.

The dolphins capered in a six-pack,
smiling and black under a shooting star,
while the enormous, low-hanging moon
tinseled the liquid licking at my doorstep.

This buzzsaw of mirror-shard delirium
clips the wings of my spoken words,
leaves me speechless and unkind in silence.

The diamond firebird—ashes he stirs.

Hear me keening for understanding,
my love? Wait, not yet, while I paint
another sequined scrim of myself.

Here, wrap this hemp around your waist,
tighten it to breath-shortening snugness.
That shadow ahead is a warm hayloft.

We may be blinded by this blizzard,
but we need not be lost.

Patience

Night worry who

knows my question, fuse knot another.
In that plea finds it early
of mentions sex—an awkward
ache always early.
Honest sees a flapping

flag. I abandon when, prefers
arrivals, spread yellow
in leaves, sometime in next.
Swans' meanness leaves an example.

As I am possible, then he
is possible. Solace posits
another unconnects woman there.
The Moon pulls at all.

Drifting in colloid, speck
veers illumined speck, which trajectory
glitters in a murk and we live not specks.

Builds chimneys on mud slides slope,
adds height with soiled
my bricks from the bottom and he and I
divined not an apt parable.

Boy, my ignorance inflates
exponential while below the grass
breathes dirt—what does
requires your admiration.

I once found a silver coin
and lose ends in expanding odds.
Where glides alone a swan on silt,
swirls brown leaves an eddy,

sunlight reveals there again
in flags shadows' shift.

Hole in the Wall

The first is a SoMa bar,
where you're a regular
and I accompany you occasionally.

In front there are Harley hogs in rows,
gleaming with chrome and supple leather,
along with tubular elevator ashtrays,
since I can no longer smoke inside.

We push through a black leather curtain,
into old-school, dark, dank, stinky air,
slip past graybeards circling playing pool,
beer-sipping dirtbags, pierced punks,
fat naked accountants and glaring tweakers,
the rough and ugly, the skanky, sexy, the sad,
whispering in dangerous murmurs.

High above worn smooth plank benches,
a nine-headed wire-mesh dragon
slinks and coils across the ceiling,
glittering its Tesla ball brains
into dark recesses of fondling
and commiseration, deals and revelations.

We sit in the black shoeshine chair
in the back, chattering,
sleek twinkling elves
amongst the bears, wolves, and trolls.

The walls are plastered with posters
of the history of 20th Century sexuality—
Polaroids of asses, rock and roll flyers,
passé porn advertisements
and risqué news clippings,
risible, hot Tom of Finland machismo,
Disney stickers, and velvet paintings
of Jimi Hendrix.

My eyes flutter with a bleary tilt
of drunken, hormonal haze—
of course the drinks are cheap and strong.

"Let me reintroduce you to Ms. Tina,"
the white tongue says. "You be her bitch
through sunrise and love it."

Conversation
is as easy as asking for a flash.
Supple dark cock, sleek and strong,
a cheerful shrug with a peek.
Stroke and praise, retuck.

The DJ spins crude nostalgia with a hard
house edge, an intermittent disco beat,
sonic kitsch, lingering melodic anthems
of loss, ringing with loneliness and lust.

In the broken AM, coming down,
when the gruff billy-goat bartenders
start serving not long after dawn,

the sunlight filtering through the studs
in the leather curtain to spear linear
on the scarred velvet green,
fractured across the pool cue in my hand,

Hole in the Wall has felt like home.

o

The second is a natural formation,
a rocky outcropping carved by the Pacific,
on the coast of the Olympic Peninsula.

We woke at our mossy campsite
in the sprouting Hoh rainforest
as morning breached, hurried to drive
the mile to the ocean beach
to join Ranger Dan's tour group
for a hike along the shoreline.

Strolled past rolled-smooth rocks, lines of
massive bleached timber bunched there,
tannin in the tea-like pools beside the wood.
We inspected bulbous seaweed, examined
shiny mussels and twenty-legged sea stars,
prodded tingling anemones
who attempted weakly to paralyze us.

Out in the ebb tide,
sea stacks hulked in the white mists
like the ghosts of schooners,
while gulls wheeled above,
scolding the wind and waters.

A short hour march across the sands,
leaving footprints beside tide pools,
poking at headless baby seal corpses,
researching seaweed pods in our guidebook,
analyzing the other human pilgrims,
admiring Ranger Dan's muscular calves,
delivered us to our destination.

The formation was dark gray,
gleaming black where wet.
Its vast inner whorl was flecked
with aquatic cities of color:

green, pink, purple anemones,
red, fuschia algae, yellow barnacles,
neon orange sea stars inching up
the steep sloping sides.

This forgotten giant's arch
offered a magic portal,
an entrance to a quieter, saner dimension,
only accessible at lowest tide.

We passed through Hole in the Wall,
and part of me never returned,
a secret self left to forever wander
the shoreline of that lost beach.

o

The third is a metaphorical projection
of the guarded state of my soul.

Embarrassingly obvious, and yet
constantly a swollen cork of conflict.
I terrify in the spoken, trapped in loops,
the touch of emotion more staining
than any internalizing introvert ink.

You could not believe me,
so this is for you,
to show I remember.

How did you overlook
this gate between the battlements,
this chink in my armored scales,
this rupture oozing honest revelation,

this hole in my wall?

Kindness

Be not proud
for the art of castigation
digs its crown of thorns equally
deeply into our foreheads

a satisfaction of seconds
as in helpings or sloppy
prevents reconciliation and wedges
endless runoff from the streaming blood
dragging bemoaned particles
out the mouth of the wound

search to discover a stability
a balance of assurance a scale
teetering with wrongdoing and broken
wristwatches, ancient ceramic figurines
smashed into shards
of I'm glad you
cried and dated sweepings

how I ached in the pacing
watching the window box flowers

wilt taking the aphid attacks
personally as though signals
of interior battlements being breached
by the invading infantry
of domineering anger

hour by hour itching seethes fester
rusty resentments dragged over
glittering fields of ice bumping
across sunken steaming footprints
by frustration aflame

epic vistas are but don't feel
overwrought although tense domesticity
is the icing plastered over the salted
earth a preposterous and ridiculed
attempt to make the bitterest
roots taste like cake

silent stifled phrases of hatred
ricochet across the cluttered room
zinging bric-a-brac
tchotchkes and knickknacks
laden with soothing memories
of others' past caring and cravings
from dusty shelves tumbling

too far away to catch
into miserable irretrievability

balking at forgiveness
forgetfulness only an indication
of chemical neural abuse struggle
against the pull of sucking tar pits
of the preserved dead begging
for a soothing rush of
reassuring commiseration
negation of improbably punishing scenarios
and the dissolving acid of
hotbox night sweat under winter quilts

eating nothing but carrot
sticks and fudge-striped cookies
smoking another Marlboro Light
despite the searing throb in my left
lung and stench on my overwashed right
hand lashing out against ignorance
turbulence and mockery of my strident
ambitions of invisibility, transparency,
and immortality

curled in the sunlight
like a scrawny mouser

roiling with conflicted rage
in denial of the outward stillness
of the scolded indolent body
soft words of kindness are demanded
when we both fear how quick sharp
my claws sing at the tender of a threat

falter now firefly hostility
your mating was to little avail
I release you from this rampaging
child's lidded jar
before your brief flicker
sets in the west

hold the dagger to your
narrow ribs as I
perform my awaited act.

Sea Stack

I hope you'll meet me
in a moment of saline lucidity.

When I'm not depressed
by the distressed furniture
hulking on these sandy floorboards
like flotsam tumbled and spat ashore
from history's turbulence.

Ice-spun fog flows and ebbs
like nutrient-rich tides,
lapping at my sudden translucency.

It may mean a fight
if I'm to admit
that your insoluble boulder
describes the surge of my current.

Equipped with parasitic seed pods,
I strew my children of espionage
into the wet wind.
They report to me

with deep sea sonar
and a huge margin of error.

I peer into what happens next,
a sailor's prayer for a red moon tonight,
and wonder how many regrets
about the unfinished are required
for advanced placement in the afterlife.

I agree it's unfair to pose scenarios
with preprojected outcomes—
skewing toward a rocky outcropping
of self-fulfilling prophecy,
no matter how grotesque
the shaping desires of my ocean.

I want to camouflage
the sinkhole entrance
to this surging wound
with bleached tree branches
and detached fronds of seaweed
in the hope you'll fall in.

Lascaux

I paint a red invocation
concentrating on the children
of the Moon, a magic snare of tectiform.

In heed to my summons,
you sidled through the crowd,
approached with eyes bewildered.

What wonder as the wolf first stepped
into the yellow circle of firelight!

Take this sweet tallow rendered
from the sparse fat of my body.
Illuminate your mossy forest,
an inspiration in the mists.

It was me who sniffed out
your pebbled hormone trail
up to the cottage, the chemicals
vibrating broken spears.

I was only there for the learning.
It is disorienting to be the beloved.

Yesterday, scowling, I waved a knife,
unfunny and appropriate.
I should've marked you with a scar.

All focus has surpassed debut.
It's time for trading voices,
to settle the measure. From here,
the journey is a wander of many days.

Ample moons shall pass
before we luxuriate anew
under furs of dreary domesticity.

A mythologizing of old France.
Pain points exist in your texture
as you speak lies
about magic in the past.

A tracing of shadows'
outlines on the cavern walls.

The only ancients are ourselves.

Vita

so I was bullied by fat Jordan
his borrowed dog on a leash
then I called the police
and the garden hose coiled
hates me from the back
of my father's house
and sometimes I hid
in the antique attic
with my head brushed
by hanging clothes
which remain out of style
reading fantasy and cereal boxes
excavated by squirrels

when you wanted tales of magic
over drowsy Merlot

the moment I shook
with swiftness on a sled
sheeting ice over my head
I have a metal hip
when I hit the old poplar
in old Mrs. Goldberg's basin

and was a story read
in a dusty book by flashlight
three times maybe four
before I could call us love
and was new

what are you demanding
in waiters and Dutch checks
describe what morsel
I might have fed you
like small fruit
from a fiction which would let
this ungainly possibility fly
and confer significance
on our later nakedness

forgetting the lob of footballs
or my crush on Bucky Dent
after his two-run homer

when I have no history

no Jason's cloying cologne
entwined in his sweater

I was born this morning
when I closed my eyes

and so do I believe to adapt
dolphins sprout wings and soar
comprehending chaos in snow
staring up from the pulsing sidewalks
of lower midtown Manhattan

wanting words endlessly from my lips
fountaining in pristine droplets

of I ate crunchy curry
hamburgers in Munich

no, when I was bearded
I was nuts and drugged
and if you thought my truth
would help you comfort you
should ask the manifest someone else

The Scrivener

Elderly, more than ordinary, privately:
no materials exist for myself or by prudence.
My next method is a premature act,
tame than otherwise,
lurking beauties, promising lad.

With submission, sir, with submission.

Piratical duties knew not what he wanted.
Diseased, certain ambiguous-looking
fellows, clients, natural civility
and deference, dependent insolent.
He was a man whom prosperity harmed.
Temperate, with submission, sir.

Receiving the master's office,
pallidly neat, pitiably respectable,
incurably forlorn! Sedate humor,
erections, privacy and society
gorge cheerfully industrious.

I would prefer not to,
rising in high excitement, pillar, passion,

thrust, disarmed. Touched flute,
revolved, paramount.

With submission, sir.

Sore, deferentially,
would do another man's business
without pay.
Hermitage beckoned.
Probably he preferred it should have none.
Passive resistance, and the resisting one
perfectly harmless in his passivity.
Means no, intends involuntary.

He is useful to me.

Befriend, humor, strange willfulness,
sweet morsel, passiveness,
opposition, elicit some angry spark.
Mastered, just step
behind his screen, rousing.
I burned to be rebelled against again.

You will not?

I prefer not.

Repulsed agreeably to the laws
of magical invocation,
at the third summons,
respectfully retribution intended.
Acknowledge out of compliment,
doubtless to their superior acuteness
to be dispatched. Would refuse,
reconciled, freedom unalterableness.
He was always there, most precious, safe.

Avoid falling into sudden spasmodic
passions with him.
Stipulations inadvertently common,
infirmities of our nature:
perverseness, unreasonableness
repulse inadvertence.

Celebrated preacher resisted something
inserted from the inside,
in his shirt sleeves, and otherwise
in a strangely tattered dishabille.
Preferred not admitting me,
I had better tenanting,
withal firm and self-possessed,
incontinently did as desired.
Impotent rebellion,
but unmanned me.

Unmanned when he tranquilly permits
his hired clerk to dictate to him,
order premises, shirt sleeves,
and in an otherwise dismantled amiss,
not to be thought of for a moment
an immoral person.

Decorous nudity, secular occupation
violate the proprieties, hindrance I inserted.

Impress of a lean, reclining form,
morsel of cheese, bachelor's.
What miserable friendlessness and loneliness
are here revealed! His solitude
overpowering, stinging, melancholy,
bond of a common humanity,
fraternal sons of Adam.

Misery hides aloof pale form,
appeared to me laid out,
among uncaring strangers,
in its shivering winding sheet,
attracted holes.

Old bandanna handkerchief,
quiet man like other men.

Who he was:
pallid haughtiness, austere reserve,
awed tame compliance.

Feared to ask him.
Coupling enlists our best affections:
succor, disorder, give alms to his body,
accomplish what I would do.

His services, I could assist him,
be happy to do so,
willingly help, want of aid.
I am not going to ask you to do
anything you would prefer not to do.
I feel friendly towards you, waiting.

At present weak, nettled, disdain,
perverseness. Good usage received,
felt something superstitious
knocking at my heart, forbidding,
denouncing me for a villain,
forlornest of mankind.

Familiarly, behind his screen
revealing, as a friend, help.
At present I'd prefer him,
I'd prefer preferences,
I'd prefer to withdraw involuntarily.

My contact with the scrivener
had already and seriously affected me
in a mental way. What further and deeper
aberration may produce efficacy,
deferentially.

With submission, sir,
prefer enabling him to assist,
got with submission respectfully.
Here queer, he would but prefer.
Withdraw, if you prefer.

Asked whether I would prefer,
roguishly, involuntarily demented man
turned the tongues, if not the heads
of myself and clerks.

Dismission, his stay with me.
I was touched, abstaining.
Embrace earthy, less inflexible urgings.
Fixture in my chamber,
millstone to me, not only useless
as a necklace, but afflictive to bear.
Occasioned me uneasiness alone,
absolutely alone in the universe.
Tyrannized, offered to assist him.

You finally quit me.
Touched his shoulder.
I would prefer not, he replied,
with his back still towards me.

You must.
I am apt to be very reckless in affairs.
Slip your key underneath the mat,
so that I may have it in the morning.
I can be of any service to you.

He was more a man of preferences
than assumptions, all alive.
Kept veering about, excited.

Pocket to produce my own intent excitement,
screened absent-mindedness.
Still I tried the knob.

Yet a certain melancholy mixed with this;
I was almost sorry for my brilliant success
fumbling have left there for me.
Not yet; I am occupied.

For me, help nervous resentment,
demonstrations. He and I were alone,

dreadfully incensed, wildly excited.
Certainly no man could possibly deplore
more than the actor himself,
the subject entirely unhallowed
by humanizing domestic associations.

Old Adam of resentment rose in me,
tempted, grappled him and threw him,
that ye love one another.
Jealousy's indulged, abated courtesy,
munched his noon apple.

Billeted upon me, persecute.
I never feel so private as when I know
you are here. I feel it penetrate
to the predestinated purpose of my life.
I am content, unsolicited.

Uncharitable remarks obtruded upon me
by my professional friends
who visited the rooms.
Constant friction of illiberal minds,
sinister observations touching
my whereabouts.
Immovable in that position,
deeply occupied.

Wholly unemployed, request him.
Tranquilly decline.
Circle, whisper of wonder,
reference to the strange creature I kept
at my office, keep occupying
my chambers, denying my authority,
scandalizing my professional reputation.

Soul and body together,
savings outlive right
of his perpetual occupancy.

Intruded their relentless remarks
upon the apparition in my room.

Gather all my faculties,
intolerable incubus.

Will you go home with me now?
But my dwelling, our leisure,
at present I would prefer not
to make any change at all.

I had now done all that I possibly could.

My own desire, rude persecution,
quiescent fugitive trembling,
removed to the Tombs.

Peering out upon him the eyes
of murderers and thieves,
I want, so I left him.

Broad meat-like man, in an apron,
accosted me. He want.
I want you to give particular attention.
You must be prove of benefit
to the scrivener, I acquiesced.
You will find him very useful to you.

Your sarvant, sir, your sarvant,
deranged, they are always pale
and genteel-like, them forgers,
touchingly laying his hand
pityingly on my shoulder.
Socially acquainted the silent man,
yonder he lies, surrounding walls
of amazing thickness.
Egyptian, strange magic,
something prompted me to touch him.

Lives without dining,
parting with the reader,
interested, awaken curiosity
I am wholly unable to gratify.

How true it is I cannot now tell.
Certain strange, suggestive interest,
subordinate clerk in a Dead Letter Office
suddenly removed by a change
in the administration.

I cannot adequately express the emotions
which seize me.

Conceive a man, prone,
continually handling flames,
takes a ring stifled
by unrelieved calamities.

Ah.

Hoodwinked

Hoping to posit the preposterous
despite the crosswalk
and the missed alarm of last.

My fascist fantasia marches
in reveries, otherwise naked
but for jackboots and shadows
of stretching corridors of mistrust.

This window is a freeway overpass
where the Greek ends in *plast*
or *blast*, perhaps *phage*,
eating corpuscle terminology forgotten
in hormonal locker room haze.

Drowsing and fascinated in red,
the shedding dogs circle and yip,
offering their underbellies to my dominance,
even when desire suggests cowering
to another, ethereal authority.

This wisp is a homemade vintage,
a vigorous, deafened denial

of a practiced power latent
in the flashing codes of headlights
and tearful, bleary taillights.

Shatter the window, drink
or spill the wine, I, inebriated
on your air, your assertions,
know why I was late to wake,

and this shimmer is a stain
on the temporary glass
of the obvious.

Infectious

Buried in parcels
encased by moist, membranous stuff
is the angle of the sun warmer
than early risers.

My mother walked stiffly in a ski suit
leaving 118 lb. footprints
when she was 21.
She had my arms
and cried a Cherry Blossom queen.
Dad ran the committee.

Crepe paper quivers above the mud.
Screw it, I flamed virginity at 12,
although as much a nail biter.

JOKE
Q: How do you fit additional gays
into a bar crowded to capacity?
A: Turn the barstools upside down.

While I have something exterior to protect,
who will it be.
Tumbling down a pit into the arms of Pluto.
A brown ring of tooth marks,
on display in a decorative planter.

Belief in people's sincerity
is a fountain basin, or the angel
has not yet been swallowed.

My particular gender pulls at the meat
of my face, stretching, unsettled
under a reflection veiled by floaters—
under a gun I will admit all,
I'm safe,
I'll sign anything put before me.

Something, something up
for undifferentiation.
A battle isn't an anomaly,
and all forgot the seventh deadly sin
banners itself anger.

All that smarts.

How to fight what is
(a Japanese melody for flute)

by alignment,
to celebrate when called for.

I held a broken plastic token
in my moist hand
and radiated enough for one night
and the German on the bed
I named celebrator.

In the larger room people turned
touched and pleased, adopted.

The factors refuse change
but metamorphose when counting grains
of top-heavy grass.

My arms wouldn't lift the world
and I made manager,
staring up tall stalks from the lawn
gone to seed.

More to the story demands
a snow white flutter,
and the season has passed.

I have a cease fire
with my father but he won't tell
if he swallowed a nail.

Who looks busy
in that corner.

I loosened something,
a screw standing upright.

I'll kill to hold it safe.

Effort

This fingertip is calloused
with age and use
and can no longer call down magic
party tricks on command.

This party knows a thing
about disappointment,
a ride with tame horses,
even with the glitter and breakage.

This ride pours out his heart
into hot chocolate mugs,
then lurches and veers,
staining the kitchen.

This heart chokes on chicken bones,
whips off an odd-numbered veil,
as he squats in the muck
to seek a lost child.

This child enumerates his ears and toes
while broadcast on a static channel.
A push of a button reconciles God's armies,
but he won't lift a fingertip.

Emission

My Pomology

Beginning again with a confidence
myth requires. This fruit a heart,
shared between enlightened lovers,
brought by a serpent.

Granny untangled our roots
back to the Mayflower,
to a Greenleaf. I flower
white and futile,
in astrological opposite,
unpollinated and final.

Now, Esopus Spitzenburg,
extant ancient heirloom
called to acknowledge
genetic continuity,
delicate hand-to-hand value,
bounce ability to define both
as typical and best,
in the roseate glow
of the incoming.

I argued in adolescence
the impossibility of hubris
dynasties to delicious
standard—please.

Keeps me angry.

Macintosh, New Zealand Kiwi,
this desperate pomologist
fears a second bite,
a spell of lasting sleep
when it is too late
for first love's kiss.

Oblate spheroid—
exercise in sculptural
perspective, mottled green
overlaid with washes of rose,
themselves streaked randomly
with unwatered scarlet pigment,
think we know the apple.

Turns my fragile neck driven
by desire to present a gift
to the next teacher
of the many body, doused
with a perfumed afterthought
we call flavor.

Ejaculate

To find a place of textual joy
amidst the rabble in the rubble
requires a totem of assurance,
a tree sallying rhizome roots
to replicate the word of creation.

MIRVs of colonial spermatozoa
splatter onto rocky soil,
squirming into infertile tunnels
like a backhanded bitch slap
of tricked and necessary kindness.

We tango at the edge of the unknown,
flinging ashen coals like eggs.

Shadowed reveal of asexual reproduction—
the virus of an idea can thrive,
injecting genetic material to disseminate
into the loam of subjective subconscious,
propagating true to its conception,
and yet merely seem a pallid parody
of the parental gift of life.

My babies may always be illusory,
pale specters of unsent letters
diverted by great grunts of spilling seed,

forced into descriptive servitude,
monstrous, unsafe chittering sapiens
secreted in soundproofed attics,
unweaned from the milk of rejection,
tormented to laze in eternal cages
while thrice denied their risky beget,

but I do not love them less.

Integers

0 stares back moaning
to fill with eventual exponents
from flowing wet unnamed.
Mountains await,
forgotten where I put them.

1 is an unshared secret,
near an early home.
A pulse.
Who makes the mistakes.
I falsified my wish to be king.

2 lies of order,
of permanency of order.
Happy diamond in memory,
feigned supplicant to eternal,
always on his knees.

3—demon crawled from an underworld—
how you rend and torture:
thief in burns from an unwed;
mocking reminder
of my lost daughter.

4, patron of safety,
rests in content on a flat edge,
boring and fertile,
no place to go,
filled with my keepsakes,
unlit cigarettes
and a misplaced Key to the City.

5 wields a gleaming scimitar
on its merciless, tiring jihad.
Wait,
its art is unparalleled,
and blesses every yellow flower in a field.

6, plush darling,
quick to turn to treachery,
I pray to your fatness,
your tethered womb.
Come kiss my forehead,
leave your mark—
I remember time will parry the result.

Abstract slash 7
awkwardly invites attempt
of division
to laugh always at one's head on high.

Royalty festooned you with bells,
but keep closer,
in my pocket.

8, workhorse,
fellow in a twist,
balance of plenty.
Upstanding infinity,
of course, built without entrance.
Open your butterfly jar,
I allow to breathe.

And you, 9,
hurtful dangler of reversals,
the fodder marches forward
on the salted field.
There is space for lovely.
Unstopper the secreted bottle of the djinn,
no time to turn your head.
I need yours.

Because

it's over again here
we go anew anew angels fold
up spread blanket delicate paths forge
sunburn pillar of fire orientation
akin to weed sprouts know upside
down look who hasn't known this
which generation lay in the dark praying
an eternal a salvation didn't question
suggest righteous answer in rosebuds
and cigarette butts hand on soft cheek
laughing in corners like automobiles
well-tuned on sides of gravel road paved
over cyclical and breakthrough revolve
this never

again streak of sunset from a precise
irretrievable star pattern and scattering
molecules of love recombine and try
to get it better this time unless last time
chapter ends in a glory of wishing and
of oracle fallen haphazard and dusty ache
of growth wings interior smile twelve steps

to saving in a moment thousandth eyeblink
and never to be sure

on tiny airless island presumptuous
to like music and painful to shirk birth
duty of fingers and toes and eyes which shift
dark against sun to be true

endearing it's not all against trivia
and world risen above suffocating
amidst abstracts no bread and water
and soiled minty kisses and odor of books

on a shelf rage rage focus through pinpricks
a period at end a comma continues on no
endings extras only falling away to rain
in steaming lake on jumping fish
and sloping mud of banks apology
not accepted drop potato if there is nothing
nothing can destroy nothing at risk nothing
here and now not thing to bring home
to mother and expect praise it's nothing
don't mention it not here not now yesterday

tomorrow get them confused get confused
zero is only zero we know it takes two
to tangle and branching trinity reaching

out over water it is enough for plenty next
false circuit as it rears raze ground but that
but that I loved that I need that how could
be seared fallow to its because

no more twist circle and stand back
right here we're in for long haul
bumpy ride and there there's the next
and covered by black veil it only
could be probably green

Early AM Mysteries

Nothing remains to believe
except the possibility of belief—
lessening the definition of hope
into nothing more substantial
than bones and skin and
the terror of daybreak.

In the silence of the overnight,
the refrigerator's sudden buzzing
is a muted alarm, a warning cry
of omen and portent as I leap
from futon to coffee table to loveseat,
afraid of the ravenous piranhas
lurking beneath the surface
of the gray industrial carpeting.

I am tired
of proclamations of doom.

The damp cold is an uninvited guest
boring me with oft-repeated tales
of miseries more dire than my own.

My constant self-imposed solitude
has bewildered the boundaries
of the real and the actual,
like this snowy mountain peak
I hold in the palm of my hand.

While rainwater rushes down the slope
of my urban street transformed into falls,
the city lists, slumping alarmingly to the left,
jittering in a woozy double take.

Beautiful, glorious—I love you, Rosie—
the weather rolls in over the hills
like the foam frothed on a winter sea.

The true amazement:
that any madness intersects
with the obsessions of another,
that a common ground may
ever be reached. Yes,
I expect to be special,
but no preparation was possible
for the awestruck gape, the unique moment
of honest interpersonal human surprise.

How can we render a realistic future,
when the past is incurring reconstruction,

and the present perseveres in renovation,
a concentrating child tinging forcefully
on a xylophone of inconsequentiality.

Left lonely with retakes and mistakes,
riddling with persistent curious inquisition,
postmortem dismissals opening avenues
of interest, rabbit holes of information,
collecting and archiving elements
to build awkward structures of belief,
while circumventing the pronouncements
of Caesar, who expects his salute of flesh.

Research the names of inks and archaic
typefaces, the word for the new feathers
on a molting mallard, progress
of geographical boundaries and canals
stretching the width of home states
into dead celebrities who may still be
kicking, how to silence the ceaseless
susurrations of the cicadas, details
of unconsciously memorized minutia
must be taken on faith.

Gaps of knowledge demanding
specialized expertise—not only
can everything not be known,

there are always endless realms
of experiential information
to which I will never be exposed.

Inventing data in the trenches,
canyons of hypothesized grout
flaking in the orange sunshine
like the sloughing amberized surface
of early miracle polymers.

I cannot ford these crevasses
with the achy stiff length of my body,
or devote my life's passions to creating
Gothic suspensions of stone or steel.

Establishing a virtual analogue
to hypnotize the psyche into believing
in the level surface of the walking path
is derangement, a willful ignorance
of the possibility of strewn palm frond
underbrush and dusted branches
disguising a dug pit, footfalls
plunging onto befouled bungee sticks.

And yet the carpet is composed
of unnameable woven petroleum fibers
spun in a process I cannot describe.

Whispered answers suggest themselves,
wapiti, grafted seedless grapes, Marisa Tomei,
the opposition of stalactite and stalagmite,
chunky cherubim and terrifying seraphim,
glancing askance at the succubi
while distracted by all the incubi,
snippets of skimmed and skeined trivia
longing for an enzyme-protein connection
triggering a synthetic catalytic reaction
of what might momentarily stand as fact.

Another day has shimmered past
as today blurs to become tomorrow.

The collective scope of our project
is as generational as a cathedral.

Lust Song

Blush rumble bumble naked
taste tangle of saline
body tingle on tongue.

Wail, rail against pink tile
walls of bathroom tear down
shower curtain in collapse.

Not now. Fifteen days awaiting,
seventeen,
three passing cars cherry red in a row,
and change if ever.

Of course there's be desired hurt.
Get smeared with cold mud. Twigs.
And bleary gasped till dawn

breaks. The walls of house skin,
brittle morning sparrow song.

There's rabbit trap,
silver jaws glinting

in leafy overgrowth, unsprung
and awakened, never be

a student of fears,
flex those rippling wings.

Connection bliss,
a tentative blossom gift—

plank upon wobble hopes, liquid moxie,
blinded faith a green and still ripe present,
an uneasy

an unquiet

Here,
here are some flowers.

Have them if you want.

Abstraction

Stop pushing, the gurgling chasm
teems with eyeless gnawing creatures
and what's frothing
reeks damned import
and marsh stench.

In response to my revelation,
my mother wrote,
Reality or existence is fluid.
She is a Pisces,
and she wrote in pencil.

Standing on a lapped rock,
the rock turns out to be a turtle.
I hope the turtle dies.

No, no, great turtle, my apologies, endure.
Your execution would be a respite only,
as the world swims in turtle solvent,
ceaselessly seeking molecules to recycle.

My last dictionary already had a
frayed edge.

My grandfather had the gangrene
in his knee eaten away by a box
of maggots replaced fresh daily.
He stayed drunk for a year,
afraid of morphine addiction.
He kept his leg until his death.

What of us would survive a slippage
into the full flush of an uncontrolled present,
what would remain intrinsic, elemental?

The dishes need washing.
The ashtrays must be emptied.
The great serpent of knowledge
hisses his hunger for more.

I have wished for transparency,
throwing entirely open the borders
to the wavelengths of others' emotions.

A solution is easy,
and feels like surrender.

I'm alive: I refuse to submit
to repossession,
to the authority of ease,
to the turmoil of all.

The abstract angels brush overhead,
feathers always out of grasp—

Name it! Another dark stone
humps up
from the ethers,
temporarily stable,

teetering on the threshold
of an unreadably violent sea.

About the Author

Gene Hult was born on November 12, 1969 in New York City.

He has a BA in English/Writing from New York University, and an MA in English/Writing from the University of Denver.

Gene was the Managing Editor of the literary journal *Denver Quarterly*. He then worked in children's publishing for more than 20 years, at houses including HarperCollins, Scholastic, and Simon & Schuster, until he left as an Executive Editor to write full-time.

He has written more than 120 books published for children and young adults, mostly under his pseudonym J. E. Bright.

Since 2017, Gene has lived in the suburbs south of Houston, Texas with his dog Henry and cat Mabel.

Please visit genehult.com and jebright.com for more information.

Brighten
Press

The Power of Words to
Enlighten and Entertain

With all the many other demands on your attention in the world, we appreciate you taking the time to read this book.

We welcome you to explore our growing list of titles, which we believe will inspire, inform, and illuminate while never losing sight of offering adult and young readers intelligent amusement, engaging analysis, imaginative storytelling, and a good laugh, a good think, a good cry, and a good time.

Please visit us at brightenpress.com.

Made in the USA
Middletown, DE
04 August 2020